The Networking Workbook

Your Guide to Preparing for Any Professional Networking Event

Michelle Erfurt, MT-BC

Michelle Erfurt

Copyright © 2013 Michelle Erfurt

All rights reserved.

ISBN: 1493673998
ISBN-13: 9781493673995

Michelle Erfurt

DEDICATION

This book is dedicated to those who are new to networking and those who consider themselves to be introverts.

ACKNOWLEDGMENTS

This book could not have been written without the help of those who allowed me to interview them. Thank you so much for letting me ask you about your fears, concerns and joys.

Special thanks to:

My husband, Edward Erfurt IV. His constant encouragement helped me to push on and continue to get out there, introduce myself to people and exchange information.

Amy Kalas for her editing eye & ability to get me say what I meant to say.

Rachel See for her incredibly speedy design skills.

Kat Fulton for the resources to get this project off the ground.

Michelle Erfurt

CONTENTS

Introduction / 1

How To Use This Book / 2

ONE   Develop Your Long Term Goals / 3

TWO   Event Details / 5

THREE   About The Sponsor / 7

FOUR   Set Your Goals For The Networking Event / 9

FIVE   Plan For Your Goals / 11

SIX   How Will You Introduce Yourself? / 13

SEVEN   Conversation Suggestions / 15

EIGHT   Follow Up / 17

NINE   Personal Processing / 19

INTRODUCTION

When I first heard the word **networking**, I thought it was just meeting people and then being able to tell other people "hey, I know a guy who...". But I learned that meeting a bunch of people really doesn't get you anywhere. It wasn't until I gained the ability to listen and speak with others that things developed.

I learned networking means more than just making a connection with someone. Networking is about building a relationship with someone where there is a mutually beneficial exchange of information & support. Because the magic happens when that exchange occurs. THAT'S when you really get to grow professionally when and opportunities become available to you. And, that's when you get to be of service to others and share what you have to offer.

I believe one of the biggest challenges people have when it comes to networking is taking that first step to begin the networking process. The first step can be different for many people: You may feel nervous about attending ANY networking event. You may have hesitation when it is time to approach someone and introduce yourself. You may feel uncomfortable talking about yourself to strangers. No matter what your particular first step happens to be, passing over that hurdle can be tough. But once you do, you will be on your way to building long lasting relationships and positive career opportunities.

That's why I created The Networking Workbook. This workbook provides a step-by-step guide to prepare you for any networking event. When you feel prepared, your confidence will be higher. Once these worksheets are complete, they will also serve as a resource for you to look back on as you groom your contacts. Networking will become second nature for you once you follow these preliminary steps and soon you will be able to boldly walk into any networking situation.

HOW TO USE THIS BOOK

These worksheets will serve as a resource for you both before and after your networking event. It's best to hang on to them in the way that makes the most sense to you. You could photocopy, scan or create a spreadsheet of each worksheet so that you can use, store and recreate them easily at a later time.

The worksheets provide different ways for you to collect and organize information you've gathered from a networking event. Some have questions with space for you to fill in a short answer and other have a space for you to check off. Some worksheets have a simple list and you can circle the answer.

You'll also find places throughout the book where I use the term 'event'. I use it to mean a networking occurrence. This could mean a pre-planned meeting with a small group of people, an informal networking happy hour at a nearby bar, a big reception at a national conference or even an informal one-on-one meeting at a coffee shop to meet a colleague for the first time. Don't be afraid to fill out these worksheets for an event that seems small or insignificant. In the world of networking anything is possible... that small event could still lead to great things. At times, an individual networking event can pop up of the blue, like being introduced to an important person from a partnering company while you're at work. If this happens, then fill out these networking sheets after the fact so that you have a record of what happened and a plan for the future with this contact.

1. DEVELOP YOUR LONG TERM GOALS

Before you step into a networking event, it's important to explore what you envision for your business, career and personal life. Step back and look at your long term goals. This will allow you to focus on exactly what you want to gain from a networking event. While the questions asked in this worksheet are not specific to an actual networking event, they will help you understand your dreams and desires so that you know what your purpose is for attending networking events.

1. DEVELOP YOUR LONG TERM GOALS WORKSHEET

Your business:
What is your business' mission statement?
What are your current services/products?
What are your future service/product ideas?
What is your ultimate dream for your business?
Who will benefit from the services/products you provide?
Who are the people who can connect you to your customers?
Who are the people who can teach you to provide better services/products?
Why are you in business?

Your career:
What is your professional mission statement?
What are your best skills?
What are the skills you want to further develop?
What is your ultimate dream for your career?
Who will benefit from your professional skills/expertise?
Who are the people who can connect you to your customers?
Who are the people who can teach you further develop your skills?
Why are you in this career?

Your personal life:
What is your personal mission statement?
What is your ultimate dream for your life?
What makes you feel the most fulfilled?
What leaves you feeling unfulfilled?
Who can you help in your life?
Who are the people who can teach you to further enhance your life?
What do you love?

2. EVENT DETAILS

Your first networking event is next week and already the excitement is building. So, let's get started! This first worksheet is the place to list all of the basic details for this event. It may seem unimportant to determine how long it will take to get to your location, but it will help you plan your day so that you are not in a hurry to get ready or surprised by rush hour traffic. Not every event requires an RSVP, but I've added a reminder for you just in case. Some events are recurring (for example: a local professionals networking breakfast) and some may just be a one-on-one meeting. Some events may also be more formal than others, but I encourage you to fill out workbook sheets even for the most informal meeting so that you can feel confident throughout your experience.

2. EVENT DETAILS WORKSHEET

Name of event:

This event is:
    __ a large group   __ a medium sized group
    __ a small group   __ 1:1 meeting

This event occurs:
    __ monthly   __ weekly
    __ annually   __ one time

If this event is recurring, does it always take place in the same location?
    __ yes   __ no

Location of event:

Directions:

How long it'll take to get there:

Time of event:

Attire for the event: business formal / business casual

Will food be provided?: appetizers / drinks / dinner / dessert / not sure

Did you remember to:
__ RSVP
__ Pay entrance fee, if applicable
__ Schedule this information in your calendar
__ Set an alarm on your calendar
__ Pack business cards / brochures

3. ABOUT THE SPONSOR

Take time to research the host of this event, both the individual person responsible and the company as a whole. Usually at group networking events attendees are encouraged to wear name tags that often also state the company with whom you are employed. Since you've done your homework, you'll be able to identify and meet the person/company who put this event together.

You may be able to learn about the company's CEO through their website and LinkedIn. The CEO may or may not be in attendance but it's still good to know in case that person's name comes up in conversation.

Becoming familiar with the company's mission will help you understand the core values of their business and see if they align with yours. If you find similarities then they may be good candidates for growing a future partnership.

Make a list of the other people who will be at this event. This list may be of specific individuals or types of people by job title.

3. ABOUT THE SPONSOR WORKSHEET

This event is sponsored by:

Event contact person's name and title:

Email of the event contact person:

Company website url:

Company CEO and other notable administrative staff:

Company mission:

How does this relate to your mission?

Who else will be there?

4. SET YOUR GOALS FOR THE NETWORKING EVENT

You've set your goals for the future of your business. You've gathered the pertinent details about the event you're attending. Now it's time to define the reasons why you are networking and set event-specific goals. When you are in the midst of the networking event, you may encounter emotions that cause you to feel nervous and overwhelmed. It can be easy to lose focus on WHY you even signed up to attend the event in the first place and WHAT the heck you're supposed to be doing! By determining goals ahead of time, you will be setting a structure that will guide your actions at the event and help you organize the information you gather.

Start off by setting an Ultimate Goal. This is a broad goal that states what you want to get out of this event. This goal is all about YOU and what YOU want. If you need some assistance, look at the first worksheet where you developed your long term goals. This will give you some answers as to why you are attending this event.

Sample ultimate goals may include:
- To increase the amount of clients I see.
- To introduce people to the professional services that I offer.
- To educate the public about my profession.
- To increase a particular professional skill.

When you set this Ultimate Goal, be sure to define the actions behind this goal. Do you want to increase, introduce, educate, share, expand, connect, etc? Determining this action will help drive your communication during your meeting.

4. SET YOUR GOALS FOR THE NETWORKING EVENT WORKSHEET

What is your Ultimate Goal for this event?

What is your second Ultimate Goal for this event?

5. PLAN FOR YOUR GOALS

Now is the time to set a plan in motion for achieving each Ultimate Goal that you developed from the previous worksheet. Expand upon each goal by thinking about simple tasks that you can take during this networking event to help you achieve this goal. Make the tasks specific so you can be sure that you can accomplish them.

Sample ultimate goal tasks may include:

Ultimate Goal: Introduce people to the professional services that I offer.
- Task 1: Introduce self to 3 professionals from 3 different companies.
- Task 2: Tell each of these 3 professionals about the services I offer.
- Task 3: Get their contact information.

5. PLAN FOR YOUR GOALS WORKSHEET

List your first Ultimate Goal:

Task 1:

Task 2:

Task 3:

List your second Ultimate Goal:

Task 1:

Task 2:

Task 3:

6. HOW WILL YOU INTRODUCE YOURSELF?

You've done your prep work and now you're almost ready to enter the room for the first time. It is best to create a list of talking points about yourself, your business and your purpose ahead of time. Taking the time to create and practice your elevator speech (what you may say about yourself in 60 seconds) can help you avoid looking like a 'deer caught in headlights'. All of the previous worksheets have led you to plan for this introduction.

Your talking points will be directly related to your ultimate goals and tasks. The following worksheet is a basic template for you to use to develop your own elevator speech. Keep in mind that this is just a template and is intended to provide you with a framework to share your information. As you gain more networking experience, your speech will take on your own unique style and voice. The template may appear short but it is powerful. I have completed a sample of this worksheet for you to use as a guide.

Sample of this worksheet:

1. Your name: *Michelle Erfurt*
2. Who you work for: *Myself, I'm self employed*
3. The purpose of your company: *To help children grow through music therapy*
4. Ultimate goal: *Introduce people to the professional services that I offer*

Elevator Speech:
I'm (#1:) *Michelle Erfurt*. I'm a (#2:) *music therapist in private practice*. My company (#3:) *helps children grow through music therapy*. I'm here today to (#4:) *introduce people to the professional services that I offer*.

6. HOW WILL YOU INTRODUCE YOURSELF WORKSHEET

1. Your name:

2. Who you work for:

3. The purpose of your company:

4. Ultimate Goals as listed from worksheet #5:

Elevator speech template:

I'm (#1:)

I'm with (#2:)

I / We (#3:)

I'm here today to (#4:)

7. CONVERSATION SUGGESTIONS

So far, you've been able to define your goals are and how you will present yourself at the event. But, remember, networking is not a one way street; it's all about the exchange that happens between two people. The key is to engage the person in a conversation by asking them questions about themselves, listening to what they are saying and finding something that can connect the two of you together. This 'something' that connects you may be a need that they are expressing that you can fulfill, it can be a problem that they're having that you have experienced as well or it could be a shared purpose between yourselves. The next worksheet is a list of questions and phrases that you can use to get the conversation going and learn more about the other person.

7. CONVERSATION SUGGESTIONS

Starters:
- Look the person in the eye, hold out your hand, give a firm handshake and say *"Hello, I'm name and it's nice to meet you."*.
- If they introduce themselves but don't mention their company or why they're there, then ask them:
  - *"What company are you with?"*
  - *"Your name tag says you're with company xyz, are you the folks who..."* Ask if their office/store is downtown, if they work with a certain client population (children, adults, etc.), or if they're the ones with the radio commercial with the catchy jingle. Anything that allows them to say something about their business.
- When they ask how you are doing say: *"I'm well. I'm here to state Ultimate Goal"*.
- Tell people how you heard about them and give an honest compliment: *"I follow you on Facebook, I get tips on how to promote my business by following what you do with Facebook. You're share great information."*

Learning about their company:
- *"How is everything going? You seem very busy."*
- *"I'm new to town and I'm not sure I understand EVERYTHING that you do, will you fill me in?"*
- *"I feel like you guys have been in business for a while now! What's it like to be such a staple in the community?"*
  - This can lead into you mentioning that you are new to town and trying to spread the word about your business. Or, it can lead into you saying how you've been in business for a while as well.

Finding connections:
- If they say anything that resonates with you, then say it...
  - *"That's great! I also work with that client population but it's in this way..."* then, fill them in on your work.
  - *"I have been having some challenges getting the word out about services too. So far I've tried xyz with some success. How about you?"*

Getting their contact information:
- *"It has been great talking with you. Can I have your business card?"*
- *"It has been great meeting you, can I give you my business card?"*
- *"Maybe we can meet again about partnering up to promote our services together. Can I have your business card?"*

8. FOLLOW UP

Congratulations! You were successful at the networking event. But, your work is not over when the event has ended... it's actually just beginning! The next day after a networking event, email the host a thank you note. It's important to follow up with every single contact that you made. This is your opportunity to reconnect with everyone you've met, make sure they have your contact information, and begin to build relationships.

During the event, people will give you their business card. Immediately after the event, even before you drive home, take a minute to write notes on the back of each card about the individual. This will help you remember your conversation with them.

The next day, fill out a "Follow Up" worksheet for each person who is now in your contact list. Make sure to write down any ideas you have for the future with this person even if it's something that you didn't discuss with them in person. Organize these worksheets together in one place so that you can look back on them months later and you will never forget someone that you met.

8. FOLLOW UP WORKSHEET

Name:

Position:

Company name and website url:

Telephone:

Email:

Date first met this person:

Met at a: networking event / 1:1 meeting

If met at a networking event, who was the host?

What does their company do / offer:

How do you connect with them? What are your similarities?

How they may be able to help you:

Future plan ideas:

Did you remember to:
__ Email them a 'nice to meet you' note. Include in your message any future meetings together.
__ Schedule in your calendar any future follow up plans (every 2 weeks, every 3 months, etc.)

9. PERSONAL PROCESSING

Now that you've successfully made it through your latest networking event, take some time to process how it went for YOU. This will help you discover what worked for you and what you would like to do differently next time.

9. PERSONAL PROCESSING WORKSHEET

What did you think this event would be like?

What were your feelings about attending this event?

During the event, what went really well?

What was easy for you to do?

During the event, what didn't go very well?

What was the event actually like? Was it like you expected?

What were your feelings after attending this event?

If you could do it all over again, what would you change?

What did you learn about yourself after attending this event?

What did you learn about networking after attending this event?

ABOUT THE AUTHOR

Michelle Erfurt, MT-BC, is a music therapist who uses networking as a cornerstone in her career. She has worked in medical, hospice and private practice settings. She shares her thoughts on music therapy related topics at her blog: MusicTherapyTween.com and podcast: MusicTherapyRoundTable.com.

www.ingramcontent.com/pod-product-compliance
Lightning Source LLC
Chambersburg PA
CBHW081819170526
45167CB00008B/3463